St. Augustine
on my mind

Photography by Ken Laffal

FALCON®

Early-morning sunlight casts a warm glow over the graceful towers of the St. Augustine skyline.

> **❝** *There is more of new than of old St. Augustine, yet over the town hangs the serene atmosphere which comes only with calm age…. Like the gnarled cedars clinging to the windswept shores of the beaches, its roots are strong and deeply embedded in the soil.* **❞**

Federal Writers' Project

A pelican plans its next fishing expedition.

The pleasure craft *Ramblin' Rose* checks in at the Municipal Marina.

Once a Mississippi River paddleboat, the *Anastasia* now offers cruises on the Intracoastal Waterway.

A carriage tour passes the Bridge of Lions, built in the 1920s and now on the National Register of Historic Places.

A pair in need of a fare.

"You can not be in St. Augustine a day without hearing some of its inhabitants speak of its agreeable climate."

William Cullen Bryant, 1843

The bayfront promenade awaits early-morning joggers and strollers.

> *The climate of Florida is undoubtedly its chief charm. Its beauties and virtues have for a hundred years filled the homes of St. Augustine with people striving to recover from the effects of severer surroundings; it will always be a refuge.*

Edward Smith King

A bayfront streetlight is outshone.

Built around 1800, the City Gate once had heavy doors to seal off the town at night.

Multicolored coleus plants comprise an inviting entrance to the Visitor Information Center on San Marco Avenue.

In 1821, Government House served as the first state capitol of Florida. Today it houses a small museum and offices.

In late afternoon, soft light filters through the Spanish moss in the narrow lanes of the old city.

St. George Street features a wealth of historical buildings, including the Oldest Wooden Schoolhouse.

The waterwheel still turns at the Milltop Tavern, a former millhouse and now a popular nightspot.

The Old Spanish Quarter is a living-history museum, re-creating life as it was in the 18th century.

Woodworking the old-fashioned way.

A living-history performer spins wool in the reconstructed De Hita House.

A blacksmith at his forge.

66 This most ancient city of our land,... where everything recalls the past, whose very existence is a landmark of history [provokes] an earnest desire to look into that past, to draw out its secrets, and to bring back to our own minds and memories the scenes and actions of the olden time. 99

George R. Fairbanks

Old brick pavers seem to lead to bygone days.

The Prince Murat House was named after a nephew of Napoleon Bonaparte. Murat reportedly lived here around 1820.

A charmingly weathered gateway on Bridge Street opens onto a private garden.

A peaceful dawn breaks over Castillo de San Marcos, a 17th-century fortress that has never been taken by force.

“ *Emerging from the solitudes and shades of the pine forests, we espied the distant yet distinct lights of the watch-towers of the fortress of St. Augustine, delightful beacons to my weary pilgrimage.* ”

English traveler, 1817

Palmettos, pines, and grasses surround a tidal marsh at Faver-Dykes Park.

Tranquil waters and marshes provide habitat for wading birds and other wildlife, as well as opportunities for boating.

This heron makes its home at the Alligator Farm, a prime location for bird watchers.

With put-ins in Faver-Dykes Park, Pellicer Creek offers miles of scenic canoeing and kayaking.

A volleyball enthusiast stretches for a return at St. Augustine Beach on Anastasia Island.

66 The atmosphere exhilarates. On one's energies and spirits, it acts as a stimulus, so that one does not suffer from lassitude here, as is usual at the north. 99

R. K. Sewall

Bring on those 65-year-old youngsters!

A golfer tees off on the Slammer and the Squire Golf Course, within sight of the World Golf Hall of Fame.

A couple cruises Magnolia Avenue on a bicycle built for two.

Palm-thatched roofs overlooking the water create a Polynesian ambiance at the Conch House Restaurant.

Alfresco dining at Scarlett O'Hara's Restaurant.

Low tide exposes oyster bars in the Intracoastal Waterway, a shipping route that parallels the Atlantic coast.

Beyond the marshes lies Camachee Cove Marina.

Built in 1888, Flagler College was originally the Ponce de Leon Hotel, where the wealthy and famous came to escape northern winters.

Intricate woodwork, stained glass, and a hand-painted ceiling lend a unique elegance to the Flagler College dining room.

Not your typical college dormitory.

One is impressed in St. Augustine with the feeling which ancient European cities give the sensitive traveler, a sense of continuity, of being a part of the stream of life and of time from the beginning of things.

Frank Parker Stockbridge

A 208-foot-high cross marks the site of the first Catholic mass held in the New World, in 1565.

" Wandering here, one comes to think it more than a fancy that the land itself has caught the grave and stately courtesies of the antique Spaniards. "

Sidney Lanier

Ivy softens the face of the Chapel of Our Lady of La Leche at the Mission of Nombre de Dios.

Centuries of Spanish influence are evident today in the architecture and decor of St. Augustine.

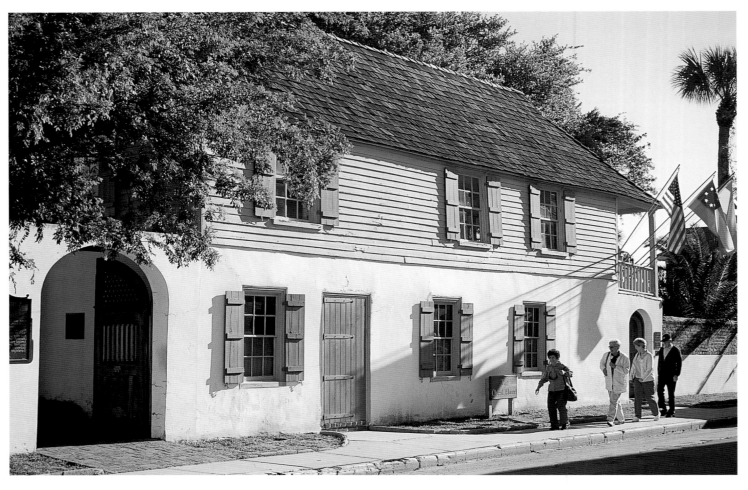

Gonzalez-Alvarez House, also known as the "Oldest House," is said to have been occupied since the early 1600s.

Statues decorate the gardens of the Oldest House.

The stark interior of the Oldest House conveys the simplicity of life in the 17th century.

Preferring shade, azaleas bloom beneath an ancient live oak at Washington Oaks Park.

An azalea blossom opens in early spring.

Live oak limbs draped with Spanish moss form a canopy over Magnolia Avenue.

Every new curve [of the river] started clouds of birds, shining white egrets, herons, roseate spoonbills, jeweled green kingfishers all clacking and rustling across in a feathered roof against the dazzling strip of sky.

Marjory Stoneman Douglas

A great egret displays its plumage as part of a courtship ritual.

Sago palm leaves emerge as one and then slowly unfold to form a ring of new growth.

❝Almost every house has its little garden, of which splendid lemon and orange trees are not the least ornaments.❞

Johann David Schoepf, 1784

A sculpture punctuates a hedge of fragrant Confederate jasmine.

Canary Island, sabal, and pindo palm trees shade a Spanish-style brick courtyard.

Subtropical plants attract butterflies to local gardens.

While the St. Augustine Lighthouse pierces the last vestiges of night, a fiery sunrise signals the start of a new day.

Built in 1874 and still in use today, the lighthouse towers above the small house once used to store fuel for its beacon.

Framed by old oak trees, the former light keeper's house is now a museum and gift shop.

12 down, 207 steps to go to the bottom of the lighthouse.

The early riser can still find a truly deserted beach.

The sun swung steadily up the sky, and they knew it was broad day because the color of the sea changed from slate to emerald-green, streaked with amber lights, and the foam was like tumbling snow.

Stephen Crane

Windswept sand contrasts texturally with coquina rock.

Low tide at Matanzas Inlet exposes coquina, a soft limestone composed of crushed shells.

A boardwalk stretches across the dunes at Butler Beach Park.

Looks like the surf's up at "A" Street Beach.

Family bonding at Anastasia Park.

Independence Day draws a crowd of sun lovers to Crescent Beach.

When the Eighth Wonder of the World is officially recognized, St. Augustine will have a just claim to consideration for her superb beaches.

A Travelogue of Saint Augustine Florida

Soothed by the surf.

Forty-three miles of beaches mean plenty of room for a relaxing stroll.

A pail, a shovel, and a mighty big sandbox.

> *The appearance of the town is rather romantic, especially when the Spanish Fort, which is quite a monument of ancient architecture, opens to the view.*

John James Audubon

The guns of Augustine.

The oldest masonry fort in the United States, Castillo de San Marcos was built beginning in 1672.

An active military post until 1900, the Castillo has been occupied by armed forces of the Spanish, the British, the Confederate States of America, and the United States.

Cannon firing demonstrations are a popular part of summer weekends at the fortress.

Re-enactors march through town at dusk during Spanish Nightwatch, an event held every June.

Antique cycle enthusiasts show off their classic models at the annual Victorian Spring Celebration.

A group arrayed in Victorian costumes poses for a portrait at Government House.

A lacy parasol complements a fashionable lady's attire.

" I am stopping for two or three days at the 'oldest city in America'— two or three being none too much to sit in wonderment at the success with which it has outlived its age. "

Henry James

Built in 1888, the luxurious old Hotel Alcazar has been transformed into the Lightner Museum and City Hall.

Sculptures decorate the interior of the Lightner Antiques Mall, formerly part of the Hotel Alcazar.

In what was once the swimming pool of the old Hotel Alcazar, the new Cafe Alcazar serves lunch.

Artifacts of Victorian high society are displayed at the Lightner Museum.

Lined with small shops and cafes, St. George Street is the main pedestrian thoroughfare in town.

A mime makes a fashion statement.

The narrow streets and lanes of historic downtown are pedestrian-friendly.

Who needs a rhythm section?

" The place is so pleasant, that those which are melancholicke, would be inforced to change their humour. "

Rene de Laudonniere, 1564

More than 100,000 items crowd the Oldest Store Museum, a re-creation of a late-19th-century general store.

People came to the store for everything—to shop, to have teeth pulled, and to have spectacles... fitted. They could even get a haircut and, while they were at it, catch up on all the news.... Much of the town's—and Florida's—history was planned and discussed around the store's potbellied stove.

Linda R. Wade

Semiformal attire?

Bougainvillea frames the small boutiques and galleries of Charlotte Street.

Memorial Presbyterian Church, on Sevilla Street, was built by Henry Flagler in 1890 in memory of his daughter.

Stained glass from Trinity Parish Church.

Hundreds of artisans from Italy and elsewhere toiled around the clock to complete Memorial Presbyterian in exactly one year.

Evening traffic passes the Basilica-Cathedral in downtown St. Augustine.

Zorayda Castle is a reproduction of the Zorayda Tower in the Alhambra, a famous castle in Old Granada, Spain.

" Marvelously enough, St. Augustine, at least in its central downtown section, still looks like an ancient city. Therein lies its charm.... "

Frank Parker Stockbridge

Dawn paints the sky over Anastasia Island.

Large boulders strengthen the seawall at Matanzas Inlet.

Shortly after sunrise, the beach belongs to walkers and shorebirds.

A sea turtle hatchling finds its way to the water.

❝ They could see, through the Inlet of blue, blue water with the golden sand on both shores, the froth of the breakers and, beyond them, the swells of the sea.❞

Mary Mellon McClung

The St. Augustine Beach Pier lures those hoping for a good fish tale.

Quick work with a net assures a crab dinner at Guana River Park.

A fisherman prepares to cast for mullet, the preferred bait fish.

Sabal palm, the state tree of Florida, survives a landscape made harsh by sea and wind.

Sea breezes riffle the sand at Anastasia Park.

Waterfront homes overlook an expanse of unbroken sand at Crescent Beach.

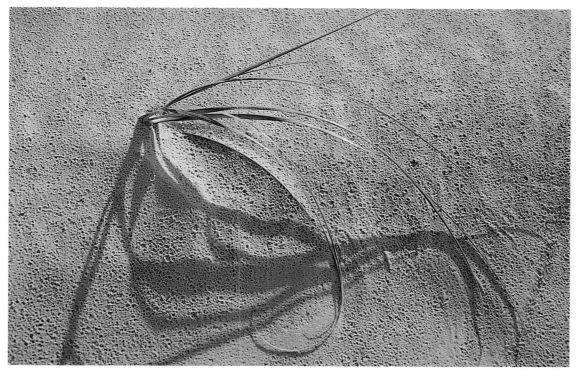

Dune vegetation takes root in the shifting sand.

Boards of every description can be found at the Surf Station on St. Augustine Beach.

With year-round surfing, St. Augustine has produced some top national competitors.

The unmistakable facade of a popular surf shop.

" Surf's up! That call can move bodies off a beach as fast as 'abandon ship' motivates people off a boat. "

Karen Harvey

A duo takes a well-deserved break after building a Mayan Temple on the shores of Crescent Beach.

A surfer scopes the wave action at Crescent Beach.

Rendezvous on "A" Street Beach.

A para-sailor finds aerial adventure off the coast of Vilano Beach.

“ St. Augustine is as addicted to water sport as any seaside city, and supports it in all forms from boogie boarding to windsurfing. ”

Karen Harvey

Steady ocean breezes make sailboarding popular.

With the help of a brisk tailwind, a sailboat heads toward the mouth of the inlet and the open sea.

The Bridge of Lions lights up for the holidays.

> *It is the city's colorful past rather than its plush hotels or myriad recreational activities that draws tourists.*
>
> Gary Fishgall

Keeper of the bridge.

Hope springs eternal at the Fountain of Youth.

" *The Fountain of Youth, supposedly one of the spots visited in 1513 by Ponce de Leon in his search for eternal youth, is, of course, a figurative expression; but enclosed in a mission-like grotto of coquina rock and overhung with ferns is a deep and ancient well whose cool waters, if no elixir, are at least capable of refreshing the weary traveler.* "

Federal Writers' Project

A diorama depicts Ponce de Leon's encounter with the Indians as he discovered a spring
he believed to be the Fountain of Youth.

An old stone building houses the gift shop for the Fountain of Youth.

Ancient pottery and lush vegetation decorate the park-like grounds of the Fountain of Youth.

A peacock rests at the foot of a statue.

Ripley's Believe It or Not Museum is filled with the strange and wondrous discoveries of world traveler Robert Ripley.

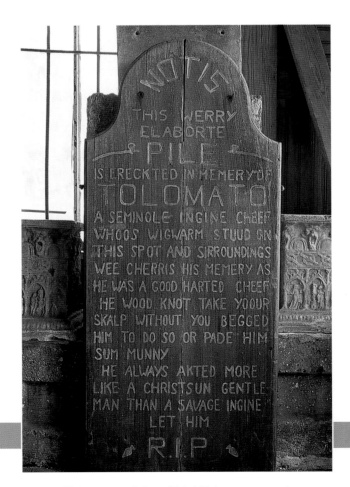

This memorial to Chief Tolomato stands in the Old Drugstore.

The inscription on the gravestone reads:

AT REST.
JOHN B. STICKNEY.
BORN IN LYNN, MASS.
MAY 25 1832.
GRADUATED
AT YALE COLLEGE 1856
DIED IN WASHINGTON D.C.
NOV. 5 1882.

STICKNEY

The tale of old Judge Stickney is one of many spooky stories told by guides on the popular Ghost Tour.

Recently renovated to its turn-of-the-century glory, the Casa Monica Hotel is a downtown landmark.

A statue of Don Pedro Menendez de Aviles, founder of St. Augustine, watches over the Casa Monica.

" After the salvation of my soul, there is nothing in this world that I desire more than to see myself in Florida. "

Pedro Menendez, 1574

Lawn chairs fill Constitution Plaza as zydeco enthusiasts listen to a summer evening concert.

A harpist adds harmony to a colonial festival.

As the rhythmic drumming quickens, an Indian dancer becomes a blur of movement and color.

An Indian powwow draws dancers of all ages.

A youngster takes a whirl on the antique carousel at Davenport Park.

Local artwork decorates the Swing Playground.

A young re-enactor flashes a timeless smile at the Spanish Nightwatch.

Kenny Pierce, better known as "Mr. Potbelly," mans the counter at his movie theater of the same name.

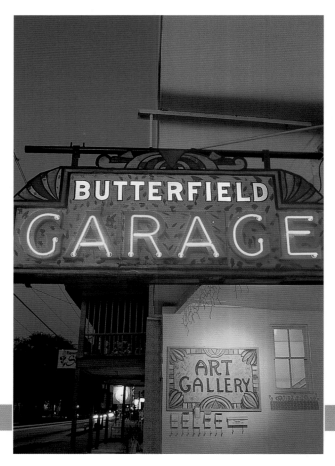

Once a car-repair shop, Butterfield Garage is now a gallery offering "full-service art."

Artist John Richards puts the finishing touch on one of his unique wire and vinyl paper lamps.

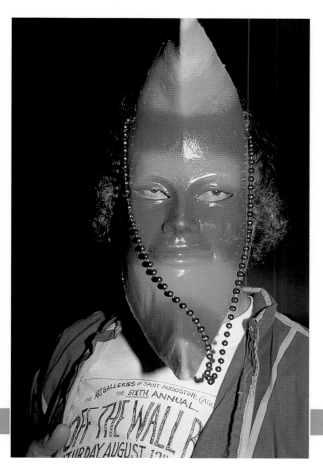

Incognito at the "Off the Wall Ball."

" Florida has always provided a home for individualists....."

John Ames

A vintner checks for clarity and color at the San Sebastian Winery.

Enjoying the finished product.

New Orleans-style wrought iron enhances the bayfront home of the A1A Aleworks and Habana Village Cafe.

There's no arguing with the prices at this antique shop.

The ambiance of an open-air market entices pottery shoppers to explore "Market to Market."

Wrought iron lanterns cast a warm glow over the arched entrance to the Columbia Restaurant.

Artist Charles Dickinson captures
a courtyard on canvas.

*" One has to be in St. Augustine some
time before one realizes, as one passes by
these commonplace exteriors of whitish
houses and whitish walls, the unsuspected
beauties stretching back within. "*

Sidney Lanier

A cat considers whether to nap on the ancient pavers or among the flowers in this serene downtown courtyard.

Dahlberg daisy

Hibiscus

Mimosa

Plumbago

Echinacea

Lantana

" The beauty of the natural world lies in the details. "

Natalie Angier

Come face to face with this prehistoric-looking creature at the Alligator Farm.

Though alligators... naturally repel us, they are not mysterious evils. They dwell happily in these flowery wilds, are part of God's family, unfallen, undepraved, and cared for with the same species of tenderness and love as is bestowed on angels in heaven or saints on earth.

John Muir

A scarlet macaw guards the entrance
to the Alligator Farm.

Although they sometimes seem permanently immobile, alligators can surprise unwary prey with their quickness.

The serenity of Crescent Beach enhances a lovely sunrise.

Seagulls flock to breakfast shortly after dawn.

Distant showers can't dim the pleasure of a sightseeing cruise aboard the *Victory III*.

In a flat country stretches of water are doubly welcome. They take the place of hills and give the eye what it craves.

Bradford Torrey

Traditional Southern-style homes featuring upstairs porches line Marine Street.

A breezy porch adds to the appeal of Westcott House, a bed-and-breakfast inn.

acknowledgments

Pages 3, 17, 86, and 93 quotes from *Seeing St. Augustine,* compiled and written by the Federal Writers' Project, Works Progress Administration. St. Augustine: The Record Company, 1937.

Page 5 quote from *Letters of a Traveller; or, Notes of Things Seen in Europe and America,* by William Cullen Bryant. New York: George P. Putnam, 1850.

Page 7 quote from *The Southern States of North America,* by Edward Smith King. London: Blackie and Sons, 1875.

Pages 13 and 61 quotes from *The History and Antiquities of the City of St. Augustine, Florida,* by George R. Fairbanks. Gainesville: University of Florida, 1975. Facsimile reproduction of 1858 edition.

Page 22 quote from *Sketches of St. Augustine with a View of Its History and Advantages as a Resort for Invalids,* by R. K. Sewall. New York: George P. Putnam, 1848.

Pages 27 and 67 quotes from *So This Is Florida,* by Frank Parker Stockbridge and John Holliday Perry. Jacksonville: John H. Perry Publishing, 1938.

Pages 28 and 103 quotes from *Florida: Its Scenery, Climate, and History,* by Sidney Lanier. Philadelphia: J. B. Lippincott, 1875.

Page 36 quote from *Florida: The Long Frontier,* by Marjory Stoneman Douglas. New York: Harper & Row, 1967.

Page 38 quote from *Travels in the Confederation, 1783–1784,* by Johann David Schoepf, translated and edited by Alfred J. Morrison. Philadelphia: William J. Campbell, 1911.

Page 44 quote from *The Open Boat and Other Stories,* by Stephen Crane. New York: Doubleday & McClure, 1898.

Page 48 quote from *A Travelogue of Saint Augustine Florida.* St. Augustine: The Record Company, 1931.

Page 50 quote from *Audubon in Florida,* by Kathryn Hall Proby. Coral Gables: University of Miami Press, 1974. Originally from *Ornithological Biography, or an Account of the Habits of the Birds of the United States of America,* Vol. II, by John James Audubon, 1834.

Page 56 quote from letter to Edmund Gosse, February 18, 1905. As reproduced in *The Traveller's Dictionary of Quotations,* by Peter Yapp. London: Routledge, 1988.

Page 62 quote from *St. Augustine: America's Oldest City,* by Linda R. Wade. Vero Beach: Rourke Enterprises, 1991.

Page 71 quote from *Sheepshead Point,* by Mary Mellon McClung. Philadelphia: Dorrance & Company, 1946.

Pages 79 and 82 quotes from "Surf's Up!" by Karen Harvey, *The Compass,* a magazine of the *St. Augustine Record,* July 7, 1988.

Page 85 quote from *Historic Towns of America,* by Gary Fishgall. New York: Mallard Press, 1992.

Page 99 quote from *Speaking of Florida,* by William L. Pohl and John Ames. Jacksonville: University of North Florida Press, 1991.

Page 105 quote from *The Beauty of the Beastly,* by Natalie Angier. Boston: Houghton Mifflin, 1995.

Page 106 quote from *A Thousand-Mile Walk to the Gulf,* by John Muir. Boston: Houghton Mifflin, 1916.

Page 109 quote from *A Florida Sketch-book,* by Bradford Torrey. Boston: Houghton Mifflin, 1924.

Page 112 quote from *The Travels of William Bartram,* by William Bartram. Philadelphia: James & Johnson, 1791.

Design, typesetting, and other prepress work by Falcon Publishing, Inc., Helena, Montana.

Printed in Korea.

Library of Congress Control Number: 00-136054

ISBN 1-58592-096-7

For extra copies of this book please check with your local bookstore, or write Falcon®, P.O. Box 1718, Helena, MT 59624, or call toll-free 1-800-582-2665.

Visit our web site at www.Falcon.com.

Front cover photos:
Castillo de San Marcos
Marble statue at Bridge of Lions

Back cover photos:
St. Augustine skyline
Great egret
Carousel at Davenport Park
Coquina at Matanzas Inlet

Series editor: GAYLE SHIRLEY
Design and layout: LAURIE GIGETTE GOULD
Text research: SUSAN R. PARKER

Anticipating another lovely day together.

How happily situated is this retired spot of earth! What an elisium it is!

William Bartram, 1791